50 Patterns of Paisley

Easy to Complex Designs for both Kids and Adults.

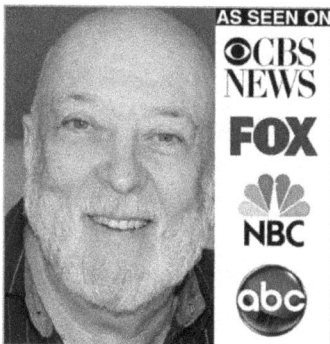

Richard Wineberg
Life Coach, Artist,
Author, Publisher,
Dancer, Grandfather

"Imagine dancing to the rhythm of your own life, not stuck in any rut, not tripping over yourself, knowing what you want and choosing to live your Purpose from the inside out.

It is my wish that you should taste, feel and be your Purpose.

Coloring books are a great form of art therapy. Let go of stress, relax, find your inner child and creativity to grow your sense of joy.

It's always time to dance..."

I0133216

1 Register and get your FREE pdf of Coloring Pages at www.DancingWithYourLife.com And check out the full range of our books and products while you're there.

Also

2 Send us a photo of your proudest colored page from one of our coloring books. The best ones selected each month will be posted on our web site. These winners will get their choice of a free coloring book Email: support@DancingWithYourLife.com

ISBN 978-0 9944230-0-9

Published by Seshat Publications
13/56 Carl Street, Woolloongabba Qld 4102 Australia
Web: www.SeshatPublications.com
Email: Support@SeshatPublishing.com

Printed by CreateSpace

Compilation and design by Richard Wineberg
Email: rkw@RichardWineberg.com

100

CALM

ART THERAPY

CREATIVITY

INNER CHILD

JOY

SATISFACTION

RELAXATION

STRESS RELIEF

FUN

MINDFULNESS

ACHIEVEMENT

Getting started...

Each page is printed only on the right hand side. It helps stop bleeding or hand pressure affecting the next drawing.

Colored pencils and crayons are fine to use.

If you are planning to use wet markers, pens or watercolor paint, please place a sheet of paper or cardboard under your current page. It's also a good idea to avoid excessive wetness.

Start on any page you like. There's no fixed order.

Enjoying the process...

Just relax and have fun with the coloring process.

It's OK to:
✓ Add your own creative lines or drawings.
✓ Add color outside lines for contrast effect.
✓ Leave areas uncolored for creative effect.

Sharing this coloring book...

Sharing with your grandchildren or children enhances the creative experience and relationship for you both.

Artists and Writers ...

Often lose track of time and awareness outside of their work. If you should suddenly become aware of this sensation take notice of how calm and unstressed you are. Acknowledge the joy, the inner child, the creativity and keep coloring.

*"There are no lines in nature,
only areas of colour,
one against another."*

Edouard Manet

"Clairvoyants can see flashes of colour,
constantly changing, in the aura that surrounds
every person: each thought, each feeling,
thus translating itself in the astral world,
visible to the astral sight."

Annie Besant

*"Man needs colour to live;
it's just as necessary an
element as fire and water."*

Lernand Leger

"If you take myth and folklore,
and these things that speak
in symbols, they can be interpreted
in so many ways that although
the actual image is clear enough,
the interpretation is infinitely blurred,
a sort of enormous rainbow of every
possible colour you could imagine."

• Diana Wynne Jones

"I know that if odour were visible,
as colour is, I'd see the summer
garden in rainbow clouds."

• Robert Bridges

"Part of my preparation is I go
and ask the kit man what
colour we're wearing -
if it's red top, white shorts,
white socks or black socks.
Then I lie in bed the night
before the game and
visualise myself scoring goals
or doing well."

- Wayne Rooney

"I put some red stuff on my mouth and cheeks
so I look healthy ~ any old red lip pencil and
a lip colour from Dr. Hauschka in a crushed berry
tone. I never put anything on my eyes,
or I look like Joan Crawford."

• Jane Birkin

"There are people who can achieve huge success in life, while adding a bit of fun and a splash of colour to this increasingly grey world."

• Peter James

"Stuart Hall was an utterly unique figure.
Although he arrived at the age of 19
from Jamaica and spent the rest of his life here,
he never felt at home in Britain.
This juxtaposition was a crucial source
of his strength and originality. Because of his
colour and origin, he saw the country differently
~ not as a native, but as an outsider."

- Martin Jacques

*"Pure drawing is an abstraction.
Drawing and colour are not distinct,
everything in nature is coloured."*

- Paul Cezanne

"When I have kids, when I have a family
and nieces and nephews,
I'm gonna teach them to love more
and be kinder and to not judge someone
by the colour of their skin or any other thing."

- Melonie Diaz

"Even if you don't like colours,
you will end up having something red.
For everyone who doesn't like colour,
red is a symbol of a lot of culture.
It has a different signification but never a bad one."

• Christian Louboutin

"The divisions of Perspective are 3,
as used in drawing; of these,
the first includes the diminution
In size of opaque objects;
the second treats of the diminution
loss of outline in such opaque objects;
the third, of the diminution and loss of colour
at long distances."

- Leonardo da Vinci

*"If you love someone, you love someone.
It doesn't matter; age, colour, c'mon!"*

• Sam Taylor-Johnson

"Blue is the male principle, stern and spiritual.
Yellow the female principle, gentle,
cheerful and sensual.
Red is matter, brutal and heavy
and always the colour which must be

fought and vanquished by the other two."

- Franz Marc

"Painting is concerned with all the
10 attributes of sight; which are:
Darkness, Light, Solidity and Colour,
Form and Position, Distance and Propinquity,
Motion and Rest."

- Leonardo da Vinci

"When I hit 16, I got a scooter to ride
to school. It was bright pink,
and I saw on the ownership papers
that Jonathan Ross once owned it.
My friends slated me for it
because of the colour, but it was cool.
My father used to ride, and my mother's
boyfriend has a bike, so we're a bit of a biker family."

• Thomas Sangster

"Shadow is a colour as light is,
but less brilliant;
light and shadow are only
the relation of two tones."

• Paul Cezanne

"We should like to have some towering geniuses,
to reveal us to ourselves in colour and fire,
but of course they would have to fit into
the pattern of our society and
be able to take orders from
sound administrative types."

• J. B. Priestley

"Since we can produce all types of light
by means of hot bodies, we can ascribe,
to the radiation in thermal equilibrium
with hot bodies, the temperature of these bodies,
and thus every radiation, even that issuing
from a phosphorescent body,
has a certain temperature for every colour."

- Wilhelm Wien

"Who says soul has only one colour?"

· Joss Stone

"White... is not a mere absence of colour;
it is a shining and affirmative thing,
as fierce as red, as definite as black...
God paints in many colours;
but He never paints so gorgeously,
I had almost said so gaudily,
as when He paints in white."

• Gilbert K. Chesterton

*"Colour is what gives jewels their worth.
They light up and enhance the face.
Nothing is more elegant than a black skirt
and sweater worn with a
sparkling multi-stoned necklace."*

- Christian Dior

"The pigeon here is a beautiful bird,
of a delicate bronze colour,
tinged with pink about the neck,
and the wings marked with green and purple."

• William John Wills

"I always saw Michael Gambon wearing madly psychedelic socks, and I always thought that's it is one of the few areas where men can really express colour and have a bit of a dandyish quality to their outfit."

- Daniel Radcliffe

"You've always got to have the right blend of colour.
You'd be silly to match a yellow t-shirt with a
light green pair of trousers, you know?
You can wear different colours at the same time,
and as long as they blend with each other then it works.
That's what I like."

- Olly Murs

*"I'm trying to incorporate colour into my life.
Until recently, everything in my closet was
black, white, grey, navy or olive."*

• Jennifer Morrison

"Bad people are, from the point of view
of art, fascinating studies.
They represent colour, variety and strangeness.
Good people exasperate one's reason;
bad people stir one's imagination."

- Oscar Wilde

"Every form is a
base for colour,
every colour is the
attribute of a form."

- Victor Vasarely

"There is something terribly morbid
in the modern sympathy with pain.
One should sympathise with the colour,
the beauty, the joy of life.
The less said about life's sores the better."

• Oscar Wilde

"I think the kind of landscape that you grew up in, it lives with you. I don't think it's true of people who've grown up in cities so much; you may love a building, but I don't think that you can love I t in the way that you love a tree or a river or the colour of the earth; it's a different kind of love."

• Arundhati Roy

"I love the sea's sounds and the way it reflects the sky. The colours that shimmer across its surface are unbelievable. This, combined with the colour of the water over white sand, surprises me every time."

• John Dyer

"When I think of flavours, I think colour,
so lemon should be yellow and orange is orange."

• Dylan Lauren

"The moon puts on an elegant show,
different every time in
shape, colour and nuance."

• Arthur Smith

"I like to keep a uniform - wear a blazer,
try to keep the same colour pants;
very tailored, very fitted but still edgy."

• Theophilus London

"I think it's because it was an emotional story,
and emotions come through much stronger
in black and white.
Colour is distracting in a way,
it pleases the eye but it doesn't
necessarily reach the heart."

• Kim Hunter

"Such lovely warmth of thought and delicacy of colour are beyond all praise, and equally beyond all thanks!"

• Marie Corelli

"The purest and most thoughtful minds
are those which love colour the most."

• John Ruskin

"If you change the way you tell your own story,
you can change the colour and create
a life in technicolour."

• Isabel Allende

"I work in colour sometimes,
but I guess the images
I most connect to,
historically speaking,
are in black and white.
I see more in black and white ~
I like the abstraction of it."

• Mary Ellen Mark

"I dream a lot, in colour and in sound and scent.
Quite a few of my stories have come from dreams."

• Joanne Harris

"They tend to come out a colour called 'Pants left in wash'."

• Eddie Izzard

"Red, of course, is the colour of the interior of our bodies. In a way it's inside out, red."

• Anish Kapoor

"Everything is expressed through relationship.
Colour can exist only through other colours,
dimension through other dimensions,
position through other positions that oppose them.
That is why I regard relationship as the principal thing."

• Piet Mondrian

"In Asia, red is the colour of joy;
red is the colour of festivities and of celebration.
In Chinese culture, blue is the colour of mourning."

• Vincent Tan

"When I used to do abstract paintings at school, like everyone else, the tutor said these would make great curtains. I would always neglect the formal stuff that was going on by using colour, because colour kind of came naturally to me."

• Damien Hirst

"I'm more into, like, colour than, like,
the type of car and stuff.
I don't know much about cars,
so I'm just more into picking the right color."

• Miranda Cosgrove

"I sometimes think that what I do as a writer
is make a kind of colouring book,
where all the lines are there,
and then you put in the colour."

• John Irving

"Any colour ~ so long as it's black."

- Henry Ford

"So one day, in a fit of trying to do something different,
I just dyed my hair dark brown
and got my first role a week later,
after which I thought: 'People are closed-minded,
man! Like a different hair colour changes everything!'"

• Emma Stone

GET YOUR FREE COLORING PAGES

DON'T FORGET

Register and get your **FREE**
pdf of **Coloring Pages**
t: www.DancingWithYourLife.com
And check out the full range of
our books and products while you're there.

ALSO

Email us a photo of your proudest colored page
from one of our coloring books to:
support@DancingWithYourLife.com

The best ones selected each month will be posted
on our web site and these **winners will get their
choice of a free coloring book**

WIN A FREE COLORING BOOK

www.ingramcontent.com/pod-product-compliance
Lightning Source LLC
Chambersburg PA
CBHW081012040426
42443CB00016B/3489